Overcoming Post Infidelity Stress Disorder

Proven Techniques for Navigating, Managing, and Healing the Emotional Turmoil of PISD While Rebuilding Trust

BY

Rachele Nucci

Table of Contents

INTRODUCTION

Infidelity is one of the most devastating events that can occur in a relationship. It shatters trust, undermines self-esteem, and brings about profound emotional turmoil. For many, the aftermath of infidelity is marked by a unique set of psychological symptoms that can significantly impact their mental health and overall well-being. This condition, known as Post Infidelity Stress Disorder (PISD), is akin to post-traumatic stress disorder but is specifically triggered by the betrayal of infidelity. Understanding PISD is crucial for those who are struggling to navigate the complex emotions and psychological challenges that arise in the wake of a partner's unfaithfulness.

This book is designed to provide comprehensive guidance on overcoming PISD, offering proven techniques for navigating, managing, and healing from the emotional turmoil caused by infidelity. It also aims to assist individuals and couples in the difficult process of rebuilding trust. By the end of this book, readers will have a deeper understanding of PISD, practical strategies for coping with its symptoms, and a roadmap for moving forward in their lives and relationships.

Understanding Post Infidelity

Stress Disorder (PISD)

Post Infidelity Stress Disorder (PISD) is a term used to describe the intense emotional and psychological distress experienced by individuals following the discovery of a partner's infidelity. The concept of PISD draws parallels to post-traumatic stress disorder (PTSD), as both conditions involve a traumatic event that leads to severe psychological consequences. In the case of PISD, the trauma stems from the profound betrayal and breach of trust that occurs when a partner is unfaithful.

PISD is characterized by a range of emotional responses, including shock, anger, sadness, and confusion. These emotions can be overwhelming and persistent, often interfering with daily functioning and overall quality of life. The disorder not only affects the betrayed partner but can also have ripple effects on the relationship, family dynamics, and even social interactions. Understanding PISD involves recognizing the deep psychological impact of infidelity and acknowledging the need for targeted therapeutic interventions to aid in recovery.

Symptoms and Diagnosis

The symptoms of PISD are diverse and can vary significantly from one individual to another. Common emotional symptoms include intense feelings of anger, sadness, and betrayal. These emotions can fluctuate rapidly, leading to mood swings and emotional instability. Many individuals with PISD experience persistent intrusive thoughts about the infidelity, including vivid mental images and flashbacks of the betrayal. These intrusive thoughts can be distressing and difficult to control, often leading to anxiety and depression.

Behavioral symptoms of PISD may include hypervigilance and an exaggerated startle response. The betrayed partner may become overly cautious and suspicious, constantly seeking reassurance and evidence of fidelity. Sleep disturbances are also common, with many individuals experiencing insomnia or nightmares related to the infidelity. Physical symptoms, such as headaches, stomachaches, and muscle tension, can accompany the emotional and behavioral symptoms, further complicating the individual's ability to cope.

Diagnosing PISD requires a careful assessment by a mental health professional. The diagnostic process typically involves a detailed evaluation of the individual's emotional and behavioral symptoms, as well as their overall mental health history. It is essential to distinguish PISD from other mental health conditions, such as generalized anxiety disorder or major depressive disorder, to ensure that the individual receives appropriate treatment. A comprehensive diagnosis will consider the context of the infidelity, the individual's pre-existing mental health, and the severity and duration of symptoms.

In summary, PISD is a complex and multifaceted disorder that arises in response to the profound emotional trauma of infidelity. Recognizing and understanding the symptoms of PISD is the first step in addressing the condition and embarking on the path to healing. This book aims to provide the tools and knowledge necessary to navigate the challenges of PISD, offering hope and guidance for those seeking to rebuild their lives and relationships in the aftermath of betrayal.

The Impact of Infidelity on Mental Health

Infidelity strikes at the core of a person's emotional and psychological well-being, often leaving deep and lasting scars. The discovery of a partner's unfaithfulness can trigger a cascade of mental health issues that extend far beyond the immediate pain of betrayal. Understanding the impact of infidelity on mental health is crucial for both the affected individual and those who support them, as it highlights the need for comprehensive and compassionate care.

The immediate aftermath of discovering infidelity is often characterized by acute emotional distress. Shock and disbelief are common initial reactions, as the betrayed partner grapples with the reality of the situation. This phase is typically followed by intense emotional upheaval, including feelings of anger, sadness, and humiliation. These emotions can be overwhelming and may lead to a state of emotional numbness or detachment, where the individual feels disconnected from their emotions and surroundings.

One of the most profound impacts of infidelity is the erosion of self-esteem and self-worth. The betrayed partner may internalize the infidelity, believing that they are somehow to blame for their partner's actions. This self-blame can manifest as a relentless inner dialogue that questions their attractiveness, worthiness, and value as a partner. Such negative self-perceptions can lead to long-term issues with self-esteem and may contribute to the development of depression and anxiety.

Anxiety is a common mental health issue that arises in the wake of infidelity. The betrayed partner may experience constant worry and fear about the stability of their relationship and their ability to trust others in the future. This anxiety can be pervasive, affecting various aspects of their life, including their work, social interactions, and overall sense of security. Hypervigilance, or an exaggerated state of alertness, is also common, as the individual becomes overly cautious and suspicious, constantly scanning for potential threats to their emotional safety.

Depression is another significant mental health consequence of infidelity. The deep sense of loss and grief associated with the betrayal can lead to prolonged periods of sadness and hopelessness. The individual may struggle with feelings of worthlessness and a loss of interest in activities they once enjoyed. In severe cases, depression can lead to suicidal ideation, underscoring the critical need for mental health support and intervention.

Trust, a fundamental component of healthy relationships, is often severely compromised by infidelity. The betrayed partner may find it challenging to trust their partner again, even if the partner expresses remorse and a desire to rebuild the relationship. This loss of trust can extend to other relationships as well, making it difficult for the individual to form new connections or maintain existing ones. The pervasive sense of mistrust can lead to social isolation, further exacerbating feelings of loneliness and despair.

In addition to the emotional and psychological impacts, infidelity can also have physical health consequences. The stress and anxiety associated with the betrayal can lead to various physical symptoms, including headaches, gastrointestinal issues, and muscle tension. Chronic stress can weaken the immune system, making the individual more susceptible to illnesses. Sleep disturbances, such as insomnia and nightmares, are also common, further impairing the individual's ability to function effectively.

It is important to recognize that the impact of infidelity on mental health is not limited to the betrayed partner. The partner who committed the infidelity may also experience significant guilt, shame, and anxiety. They may struggle with the consequences of their actions and the potential loss of the relationship. Understanding the mental health impact on both partners is essential for addressing the broader dynamics of the relationship and facilitating healing for both individuals.

Ultimately, the impact of infidelity on mental health is profound and multifaceted. It affects emotional well-being, self-esteem, trust, and physical health. Addressing these issues requires a comprehensive approach that includes emotional support, mental health counseling, and strategies for rebuilding trust and self-worth. This book aims to provide the knowledge and tools necessary to navigate these challenges, offering a path to healing and recovery for those affected by infidelity.

PART I

Navigating the Immediate Aftermath

CHAPTER 1

Coping with the Discovery of Infidelity

The moment of discovering a partner's infidelity is often one of the most traumatic and disorienting experiences an individual can face. It is a profound betrayal that shatters the foundational trust of a relationship, leaving the betrayed partner in a state of acute emotional shock. This chapter delves into the immediate aftermath of such a discovery, exploring the initial shock, emotional reactions, common responses, and the importance of seeking immediate support to begin the journey toward healing.

Emotional Reactions and Common Responses

The initial shock of discovering infidelity triggers a complex array of emotional responses. The betrayed partner may experience an overwhelming wave of emotions, including disbelief, anger, sadness, and humiliation. Disbelief is often the first reaction as the individual grapples with the reality of the betrayal. The mind struggles to process the information, and there may be an initial denial or minimization of the situation. This cognitive dissonance is a protective mechanism, allowing the individual to momentarily shield themselves from the full impact of the trauma.

As the reality of the infidelity sets in, intense anger frequently follows. This anger can be directed at the unfaithful partner, the third party involved, or even at oneself for not recognizing the signs earlier. The anger is often accompanied by a deep sense of betrayal and hurt, as the individual contemplates the emotional and physical intimacy that was shared outside the relationship. This period is marked by a volatile emotional landscape, where anger can rapidly shift to profound sadness and grief.

Sadness is a predominant emotion during this phase, as the individual mourns the loss of trust and the perceived end of the relationship as they knew it. The sadness can be all-consuming, leading to episodes of crying, withdrawal, and a pervasive sense of hopelessness. This grief is not only for the relationship but also for the future that the individual envisioned with their partner. The betrayal calls into question the authenticity of shared memories and experiences, deepening the emotional pain.

Humiliation and shame often accompany these emotional reactions. The betrayed partner may feel embarrassed and self-conscious, fearing judgment from others if the infidelity becomes known. This shame can be particularly acute in cases where there are cultural or societal stigmas attached to infidelity. The individual may question their self-worth, feeling inadequate or unlovable, which can exacerbate feelings of depression and anxiety.

These emotional reactions are not linear and can fluctuate rapidly, creating a sense of instability and confusion. The individual may experience mood swings, where moments of relative calm are interrupted by intense emotional outbursts. This emotional volatility is a normal response to trauma and should be acknowledged as part of the healing process. It is essential to understand that these emotions, while painful, are valid and a natural part of coping with such a profound betrayal.

Seeking Immediate Support

In the wake of discovering infidelity, seeking immediate support is crucial. The emotional burden of dealing with such a traumatic event alone can be overwhelming and detrimental to one's mental health. Reaching out to trusted friends and family members can provide a vital support network during this turbulent time. Sharing the pain with loved ones who can offer empathy and understanding helps mitigate feelings of isolation and loneliness.

Professional support is equally important. Consulting with a therapist or counselor who specializes in relationship issues and trauma can provide a safe space to process emotions and develop coping strategies. A mental health professional can help the individual navigate the complex emotional landscape, offering tools to manage anger, sadness, and anxiety. Therapy also provides a structured environment to explore underlying issues and begin the process of rebuilding self-esteem and trust.

Support groups, both in-person and online, can be beneficial as well. Connecting with others who have experienced similar betrayals provides a sense of community and shared understanding. Hearing stories of others who have navigated the aftermath of infidelity and emerged stronger can offer hope and motivation during the darkest moments. Support groups also offer practical advice and coping strategies that can be immediately implemented.

In addition to emotional and psychological support, practical support should not be overlooked. The discovery of infidelity can disrupt daily life, making it difficult to focus on work, childcare, and other responsibilities. Enlisting the help of trusted friends and family members to assist with these tasks can alleviate some of the immediate pressures, allowing the individual to focus on their emotional well-being.

It is also essential to practice self-care during this time. Engaging in activities that promote relaxation and well-being, such as exercise, meditation, and hobbies, can provide much-needed respite from the emotional turmoil. Ensuring adequate sleep, nutrition, and hydration is fundamental to maintaining physical health, which in turn supports emotional resilience.

Ultimately, the initial shock of discovering infidelity is a profound and life-altering event. The emotional reactions and common responses, while intense and painful, are a natural part of the healing process. Seeking immediate support from loved ones, mental health professionals, and support groups is crucial in navigating this tumultuous period. By prioritizing self-care and reaching out for help, individuals can begin to stabilize their emotional state and lay the groundwork for long-term healing and recovery.

Dos and Don'ts in the First 24 Hours

The first 24 hours after discovering infidelity are critical for setting the tone of the healing process. The emotional shock and intense feelings of betrayal can make it difficult to think clearly or make rational decisions. Having a set of guidelines can help manage the immediate aftermath and prevent actions that might exacerbate the situation. This section outlines essential dos and don'ts to follow during this crucial period.

Dos in the First 24 Hours

One of the most important things to do in the immediate aftermath is to create a safe and calm environment. This might mean physically removing yourself from a confrontation with your partner or finding a quiet space where you can collect your thoughts. Taking a step back from the immediate chaos can help prevent further emotional escalation and provide the mental space needed to process what has happened.

It is also essential to reach out for support. Contact a trusted friend or family member who can offer emotional comfort and practical advice. Sharing your feelings with someone you trust can provide a sense of relief and help you feel less isolated. It can also offer a different perspective, which might be difficult to see when you are overwhelmed by your emotions.

Writing down your thoughts and feelings in a journal can be a therapeutic way to process your emotions. This practice allows you to articulate your pain, anger, and confusion without the fear of judgment. It also creates a record of your emotional state that can be useful for future therapy sessions or personal reflection.

Seeking professional help as soon as possible is highly recommended. If you already have a therapist, making an emergency appointment can provide immediate support and guidance. If not, consider finding a mental health professional who can help you navigate this crisis. Therapy can offer coping strategies and emotional support tailored to your specific needs.

Self-care is crucial during this time. Engage in activities that provide comfort and relaxation, such as taking a walk, practicing deep breathing exercises, or listening to calming music. Ensuring that you get enough rest, eat well, and stay hydrated is fundamental to maintaining your physical and mental health during this highly stressful period.

Don'ts in the First 24 Hours

During the first 24 hours, it is vital to avoid making any hasty decisions about your relationship. While the impulse to immediately end the relationship or take drastic actions may be strong, it is important to allow time for the initial shock to subside before making any life-altering decisions. Rash decisions made in the heat of the moment can lead to regret and further complications down the line.

Avoid engaging in confrontational or accusatory conversations with your partner during this period. The emotions are too raw, and such interactions can quickly escalate into shouting matches or even physical altercations. It is better to take a step back and allow both parties some time to cool down before attempting any meaningful discussions about the future of the relationship.

Refrain from seeking revenge or acting out of spite. Infidelity can provoke a strong desire for retribution, but actions taken in anger can lead to unintended consequences and further damage the relationship. Behaviors such as public shaming, destroying property, or infidelity in return will only add to the emotional turmoil and complicate the healing process.

Do not isolate yourself completely. While taking some time alone to process your emotions is necessary, withdrawing from all social contact can lead to increased feelings of loneliness and depression. Balance time alone with reaching out to supportive friends and family members who can provide comfort and perspective.

It is also important to avoid excessive use of substances like alcohol or drugs as a means of coping. While these might offer temporary relief, they can impair judgment and lead to decisions that you might regret later. Relying on substances can also interfere with the natural emotional processing and prolong the healing journey.

Finally, do not internalize the infidelity as a reflection of your worth or value. It is common to question oneself and feel inadequate, but it is essential to remember that infidelity is a choice made by the unfaithful partner and is not a measure of your worthiness or desirability. Keeping this perspective can help mitigate the negative impact on your self-esteem.

In conclusion, the first 24 hours after discovering infidelity are a time of intense emotional upheaval. By following these dos and don'ts, you can navigate this period more effectively and set the foundation for healing and recovery. Creating a calm environment, seeking support, practicing self-care, and avoiding rash decisions are crucial steps in managing the immediate aftermath. Understanding and respecting these guidelines can help you maintain your emotional well-being and approach the path to recovery with greater clarity and strength.

CHAPTER 2

Dealing with Emotional Turmoil

In the aftermath of discovering infidelity, the emotional turmoil can feel all-consuming, as if you're caught in a relentless storm of conflicting feelings. Understanding and identifying these emotions is a crucial step toward healing. It allows you to process your experience, regain control, and begin the journey of rebuilding your sense of self and your life.

Identifying and Understanding Your Emotions

The initial discovery of infidelity often triggers a whirlwind of emotions, each powerful and difficult to manage. Shock and disbelief are typically the first responses. This is your mind's immediate reaction to the unexpected and shattering news, as it struggles to reconcile the reality of betrayal with the trust you once had in your partner. You may find yourself replaying the moment of discovery over and over, unable to fully grasp what has happened.

This state of shock is a protective mechanism, allowing you to process the overwhelming information at a manageable pace.

As the shock begins to subside, anger often takes its place. Anger is a natural and healthy response to betrayal, serving as an emotional defense against the pain of being hurt. You may feel intense rage toward your partner for their actions, toward the third party involved, or even toward yourself for not seeing the signs earlier. This anger can be consuming, leading to fantasies of revenge or a desire to lash out. It's essential to recognize this anger for what it is: a manifestation of your hurt and a cry for justice and acknowledgment of your pain.

Intertwined with anger is profound sadness. The realization of infidelity brings about a deep sense of loss. You mourn not only the betrayal but also the relationship you thought you had. There is grief for the trust that has been broken, the dreams that now seem shattered, and the love that feels tainted. This sadness can lead to feelings of hopelessness and despair, making it difficult to see a path forward. It's important to allow yourself to feel this sadness without judgment, as it is a critical part of the healing process.

Fear and anxiety often accompany these emotions. The stability and predictability of your relationship have been disrupted, leading to a heightened sense of insecurity. You may find yourself questioning your future, doubting your ability to trust again, and fearing further betrayal. This anxiety can manifest in various ways, such as obsessive thoughts about the infidelity, constant questioning of your partner's actions, and a pervasive sense of unease. Acknowledging these fears is essential to address the underlying insecurities and work towards rebuilding a sense of safety and trust.

Guilt and self-blame are also common emotional responses. You might find yourself scrutinizing your actions, wondering if you did something to drive your partner to infidelity. This self-blame is often a way to make sense of the betrayal, as it can be easier to attribute fault to yourself than to accept the unpredictability of another's actions. However, it is crucial to understand that infidelity is a choice made by the unfaithful partner and is not a reflection of your worth or shortcomings. Recognizing this can help alleviate the burden of undeserved guilt and foster a more compassionate view of yourself.

In the midst of these tumultuous emotions, you might experience a sense of confusion and disorientation. The betrayal can leave you questioning everything you believed about your relationship and your partner. This cognitive dissonance, the conflict between what you thought was true and what is now revealed, can be deeply unsettling. You may find it challenging to trust your perceptions and judgments, further complicating your emotional recovery. Embracing this confusion as a natural part of the healing process can help you navigate through it with greater resilience.

Another critical emotion to identify is humiliation. Infidelity often brings with it a sense of public exposure and shame. You might feel embarrassed about the situation and worry about how others perceive you. This feeling of humiliation can be isolating, as you might avoid reaching out for support due to fear of judgment. It's important to remember that infidelity reflects the choices of the unfaithful partner and not your value or dignity. Seeking support from trusted friends, family, or a therapist can help mitigate these feelings of shame and provide the understanding and empathy you need.

Amidst this emotional chaos, there can also be moments of numbness and detachment. These periods of emotional withdrawal can serve as a temporary respite from the intensity of your feelings. While this numbness can be protective in the short term, prolonged detachment can hinder your healing process. It's essential to balance these moments with active emotional engagement, allowing yourself to process and express your feelings rather than suppressing them.

Understanding and identifying these emotions is the first step in managing them effectively. Journaling can be a powerful tool in this process, providing a safe space to explore and articulate your feelings. Writing down your thoughts and emotions can help clarify what you're experiencing and reveal patterns that might not be immediately apparent. Therapy is another crucial resource, offering professional guidance in navigating your emotional landscape and developing coping strategies.

Practicing mindfulness and self-compassion is also vital. Mindfulness helps you stay present with your emotions without becoming overwhelmed by them. It allows you to observe your feelings with curiosity and acceptance, reducing their intensity and impact. Self-compassion involves treating yourself with the same kindness and understanding you would offer a friend in a similar situation. It helps counteract self-blame and fosters a supportive internal dialogue, which is essential for emotional healing.

Identifying and understanding your emotions in the aftermath of infidelity is a challenging but necessary part of the healing process. By acknowledging and exploring your feelings of shock, anger, sadness, fear, guilt, confusion, humiliation, and numbness, you can begin to make sense of your experience and move toward emotional recovery. Utilizing tools such as journaling, therapy, mindfulness, and self-compassion can provide the support and guidance needed to navigate this tumultuous period and lay the foundation for healing and growth.

Techniques for Emotional Regulation

Emotional regulation is the ability to manage and respond to intense emotions in a healthy and constructive manner. In the wake of infidelity, developing effective emotional regulation techniques is crucial to navigate the overwhelming feelings of anger, sadness, and betrayal. These techniques can help prevent emotional overwhelm, promote mental clarity, and support overall well-being.

One of the most fundamental techniques for emotional regulation is deep breathing. When emotions run high, the body's fight-or-flight response is activated, leading to increased heart rate, shallow breathing, and muscle tension. Deep breathing helps counteract this response by promoting relaxation and reducing physical symptoms of stress. Practice slow, deep breaths, inhaling through your nose for a count of four, holding for a count of four, and exhaling through your mouth for a count of six. This simple yet powerful technique can quickly calm your nervous system and provide a moment of respite from intense emotions.

Mindfulness meditation is another valuable tool for emotional regulation. Mindfulness involves paying attention to the present moment without judgment. It helps you observe your thoughts and feelings without becoming overwhelmed by them. Regular mindfulness practice can increase your awareness of emotional triggers and improve your ability to respond thoughtfully rather than react impulsively. Start with short sessions, focusing on your breath or bodily sensations, and gradually increase the duration as you become more comfortable with the practice.

Cognitive-behavioral techniques (CBT) are also effective for managing difficult emotions. CBT involves identifying and challenging negative thought patterns that contribute to emotional distress. For example, if you find yourself thinking, "I'm worthless because my partner cheated," you can challenge this thought by examining the evidence and considering alternative perspectives. Replacing negative thoughts with more balanced and compassionate ones can significantly reduce emotional suffering and promote a healthier mindset.

Physical activity is another excellent way to regulate emotions. Exercise releases endorphins, which are natural mood enhancers, and helps reduce stress hormones like cortisol. Engaging in regular physical activity, whether it's a brisk walk, yoga, or a workout at the gym, can improve your mood and overall sense of well-being. Physical activity also provides a healthy outlet for anger and frustration, allowing you to channel intense emotions in a productive manner.

Creative expression can be a therapeutic way to process and regulate emotions. Engaging in activities such as writing, drawing, painting, or playing music allows you to express your feelings in a non-verbal and symbolic way. This form of expression can provide insights into your emotional state and help release pent-up emotions. It's not about creating a masterpiece but about using creativity as a means of emotional exploration and healing.

Talking about your feelings with a trusted friend, family member, or therapist is another crucial technique for emotional regulation. Verbalizing your emotions can help you make sense of them and gain perspective. It also provides an opportunity for validation and support from others, which can be incredibly comforting during times of distress. Don't hesitate to seek professional help if your emotions feel overwhelming or unmanageable.

The Importance of Self-Compassion

Self-compassion is the practice of treating yourself with the same kindness, care, and understanding that you would offer to a close friend. In the context of infidelity, self-compassion is essential for healing and recovery. It involves recognizing your pain, offering yourself comfort, and avoiding harsh self-criticism.

One of the core components of self-compassion is self-kindness. This means being gentle with yourself in moments of suffering rather than harshly judging yourself. When dealing with the fallout of infidelity, it's easy to fall into the trap of self-blame and negative self-talk. However, it's important to remember that infidelity is a choice made by your partner and does not reflect your worth or value. Practice speaking to yourself with kindness and understanding, acknowledging that you are going through a difficult experience and deserve care and support.

Another key aspect of self-compassion is common humanity, which involves recognizing that suffering is a part of the shared human experience. When you're struggling with the pain of betrayal, it's easy to feel isolated and alone. However, reminding yourself that many others have faced similar challenges can provide a sense of connection and solidarity. This perspective helps normalize your feelings and reduces the sense of isolation.

Mindfulness, as mentioned earlier, is also a critical component of self-compassion. It involves being present with your emotions without judgment. Instead of avoiding or suppressing painful feelings, mindfulness encourages you to acknowledge and accept them. This acceptance creates a space for healing and allows you to process emotions more effectively. Practicing mindfulness in conjunction with self-compassion helps you stay grounded and maintain a balanced perspective during emotional turmoil.

Self-compassion also includes setting healthy boundaries and prioritizing self-care. This means recognizing your needs and taking steps to meet them. It might involve taking a break from interactions with your partner, engaging in activities that bring you joy, or seeking professional help. Self-care is not a luxury but a necessity, especially during times of emotional distress. By prioritizing your well-being, you reinforce the message that you are worthy of care and support.

Incorporating self-compassion into your daily life requires practice and intention. Start by being aware of your inner dialogue and actively replacing self-critical thoughts with compassionate ones. Practice self-kindness through small acts of self-care, such as taking a relaxing bath, reading a favorite book, or spending time in nature. Use mindfulness techniques to stay present with your emotions, and remind yourself that your pain is a part of the broader human experience.

In conclusion, dealing with emotional turmoil in the wake of infidelity requires a combination of emotional regulation techniques and self-compassion. Techniques such as deep breathing, mindfulness, cognitive-behavioral strategies, physical activity, creative expression, and talking with supportive others can help manage intense emotions and promote healing. Equally important is the practice of self-compassion, which involves treating yourself with kindness, recognizing your shared humanity, and staying mindful of your emotions. By integrating these practices into your daily life, you can navigate the challenging emotions of betrayal and move toward a place of healing and resilience.

PART II

Managing the
Healing Process

CHAPTER 3

Developing a Support System

In the journey of healing after infidelity, one of the most crucial steps is to develop a strong and reliable support system. This network of trustworthy friends and family members can provide the emotional scaffolding needed to navigate the turbulent aftermath of betrayal. The process of finding and relying on these individuals can significantly impact your recovery and help you rebuild a sense of normalcy and stability.

Finding Trustworthy Friends and Family

Trustworthy friends and family members are those who can offer empathy, understanding, and non-judgmental support. These individuals should be able to listen without imposing their own opinions or advice unless asked. It is essential to identify people who can maintain confidentiality and respect your need for privacy. The last thing you need is for your personal turmoil to become the subject of gossip or judgment within your social circles.

When seeking out these trustworthy individuals, consider those who have consistently demonstrated reliability and emotional maturity in the past. They should be capable of providing a safe space for you to express your emotions freely. This might include a close friend who has always been there for you, a sibling with whom you share a strong bond, or a parent who offers unconditional love and support. These relationships can serve as a cornerstone for your emotional recovery.

Opening up to friends and family about infidelity can be daunting. The fear of being judged or misunderstood can create a barrier to seeking support. However, it is crucial to remember that you are not alone in this experience. Many people have faced similar betrayals and have leaned on their loved ones for support. Being vulnerable and sharing your pain can foster deeper connections and provide a sense of relief.

Effective communication is key when reaching out to your support network. Be honest about your needs and boundaries. Let them know how they can best support you, whether it is through listening, offering practical help, or simply being present. Clear communication can prevent misunderstandings and ensure that your needs are met without additional stress.

The support of friends and family can also provide practical assistance. They can help with daily responsibilities that might feel overwhelming in the wake of emotional upheaval, such as childcare, household chores, or running errands. This practical support can alleviate some of the immediate pressures and allow you to focus on your emotional well-being.

It is also important to recognize the limitations of your support network. While friends and family can offer invaluable emotional and practical support, they are not a substitute for professional help. There may be times when their well-meaning advice or attempts to help do not align with your needs or the complexities of your situation. In such cases, it is essential to maintain healthy boundaries and seek additional support from professionals.

The Role of Professional Help: Therapists and Counselors

Professional help, particularly from therapists and counselors, plays a pivotal role in managing the healing process after infidelity. These professionals are trained to provide specialized support and guidance tailored to your unique situation. Their expertise can help you navigate the complex emotions and challenges that arise in the aftermath of betrayal.

Therapists and counselors offer a safe and confidential environment where you can explore your feelings without fear of judgment. They can help you process the trauma of infidelity, understand your emotional responses, and develop coping strategies. Professional therapy provides a structured approach to healing, enabling you to address underlying issues and work toward emotional resilience.

One of the primary benefits of professional help is the ability to gain insight into your emotions and behaviors. Therapists and counselors can help you identify patterns that may have contributed to the infidelity and explore ways to prevent similar issues in the future. This insight can be empowering, as it allows you to take proactive steps toward personal growth and healthier relationships.

Therapists and counselors use various therapeutic approaches to support healing. Cognitive-behavioral therapy (CBT) can help you challenge negative thought patterns and develop healthier ways of thinking. Emotionally focused therapy (EFT) focuses on understanding and strengthening emotional bonds, which can be particularly beneficial for couples seeking to rebuild trust and intimacy. Trauma-informed therapy addresses the specific impact of betrayal trauma, helping you process and recover from the deep emotional wounds caused by infidelity.

In addition to individual therapy, couples therapy can be an invaluable resource. Couples therapy provides a structured environment where both partners can express their feelings, communicate openly, and work toward rebuilding trust. A skilled therapist can facilitate constructive dialogue, helping both partners understand each other's perspectives and develop strategies for moving forward. Couples therapy can also address issues related to communication, intimacy, and conflict resolution, which are critical for rebuilding a healthy and resilient relationship.

Finding the right therapist or counselor is essential for effective healing. Look for professionals who specialize in issues related to infidelity and relationship trauma. It is important to find someone with whom you feel comfortable and who respects your values and goals. Many therapists offer initial consultations, which can help you determine if they are a good fit for your needs.

Online therapy and counseling have become increasingly popular and accessible, providing flexibility and convenience. Virtual sessions can be just as effective as in-person therapy, offering the same level of support and confidentiality. This option can be particularly beneficial if you have limited access to local therapists or prefer the convenience of receiving support from the comfort of your home.

In addition to traditional therapy, support groups can provide a valuable supplement to your healing process. Support groups offer a sense of community and shared understanding, connecting you with others who have experienced similar betrayals. Sharing your story and hearing from others can provide comfort, validation, and practical advice. Many support groups are facilitated by therapists or trained professionals, ensuring that the environment is safe and supportive.

Ultimately, the combination of support from trustworthy friends and family, alongside professional help from therapists and counselors, creates a comprehensive support system that can significantly enhance your healing journey. This multifaceted approach addresses both the emotional and practical aspects of recovery, providing the tools and resources needed to navigate the complex aftermath of infidelity.

Developing a support system is a critical component of managing the healing process after infidelity. Trustworthy friends and family provide essential emotional and practical support, while professional help from therapists and counselors offers specialized guidance and insight. By combining these resources, you can create a robust and resilient support network that empowers you to heal, grow, and rebuild your life.

Support Groups and Online Communities

In the journey of healing after infidelity, support groups and online communities can play a transformative role. These platforms provide a space for sharing experiences, receiving support, and gaining insights from others who have faced similar challenges. While friends, family, and professional help are critical components of your support system, connecting with others who have firsthand experience with infidelity can offer unique benefits and foster a deeper sense of understanding and solidarity.

Support groups, whether in-person or online, offer a community of individuals who are navigating similar emotional landscapes. These groups are often facilitated by trained professionals who create a safe and structured environment for sharing and support. The act of joining a support group itself can be a powerful step toward healing, as it signifies a commitment to seeking help and breaking the isolation that often accompanies betrayal.

One of the primary benefits of support groups is the opportunity to share your story and listen to others. Speaking about your experience in a group setting can be cathartic, helping you articulate your feelings and gain clarity. Hearing from others who have gone through similar experiences can provide validation and reassurance. You realize that your reactions and emotions are not unique but part of a common human response to betrayal. This shared understanding can be incredibly comforting and can reduce feelings of isolation and loneliness.

Support groups also offer practical advice and strategies for coping. Members can share what has worked for them in their healing journey, providing you with a diverse range of tools and techniques to try. This peer support can complement the guidance provided by therapists and counselors, giving you additional perspectives and resources to draw upon. The collective wisdom of the group can help you navigate specific challenges and make informed decisions about your recovery process.

In-person support groups provide the added benefit of face-to-face interaction, which can create a strong sense of connection and community. These meetings are typically held in confidential settings, ensuring that participants feel safe to share their experiences. The physical presence of others can offer a tangible sense of support and empathy, making the healing process feel less daunting.

Online communities, on the other hand, offer flexibility and accessibility. They allow you to connect with others from the comfort of your home and provide support at any time of day. Online forums, social media groups, and dedicated websites for those dealing with infidelity can be invaluable resources. These platforms often include discussion boards, live chat rooms, and virtual support meetings, offering a range of ways to engage and receive support.

One of the key advantages of online communities is their accessibility. They are particularly beneficial for individuals who may not have access to local support groups or who prefer the anonymity that online platforms can provide. This anonymity can make it easier to open up about your experiences and emotions, knowing that you can share your story without fear of judgment or recognition.

However, it is important to approach online communities with discernment. Ensure that the platforms you join are reputable and moderated by professionals or experienced individuals who can provide appropriate guidance and support. While online communities can be a source of valuable advice and empathy, they can also include unmoderated spaces where misinformation or negative interactions occur. Be mindful of the sources of information and support you engage with, and prioritize communities that foster a positive and respectful environment.

Participating in support groups and online communities can also provide a sense of empowerment. As you share your story and support others, you contribute to a cycle of mutual aid and understanding. This active participation can boost your self-esteem and reinforce your sense of agency in your healing process. Supporting others who are going through similar struggles can also give you a sense of purpose and connection, further aiding your recovery.

In addition to joining existing groups, you might consider starting your own support group or online community if you feel called to do so. Creating a space for others to share and heal can be incredibly rewarding and can help you establish a stronger support network. Whether you choose to lead in-person meetings or set up an online forum, taking this step can deepen your engagement with the healing process and provide valuable support to others.

In conclusion, support groups and online communities are vital components of a comprehensive support system for those healing from infidelity. They offer unique opportunities for sharing experiences, receiving empathy, and gaining practical advice from peers who understand your journey. By participating in these communities, you can break the isolation of betrayal, access diverse coping strategies, and contribute to a supportive and understanding network. Whether in-person or online, these platforms can significantly enhance your recovery, providing the solidarity and connection needed to navigate the complex emotions and challenges of healing after infidelity.

CHAPTER 4

Rebuilding Trust: Steps Towards Forgiveness

Understanding the Concept of Forgiveness

Rebuilding trust after infidelity is a multifaceted process that demands time, effort, and a deep understanding of forgiveness. Forgiveness is often misunderstood as a simple act of pardoning someone for their wrongdoing, but in reality, it is a complex and deeply personal journey. It involves letting go of resentment and bitterness, allowing yourself to heal, and possibly rebuilding a relationship that has been fundamentally damaged.

Forgiveness does not mean forgetting the infidelity or condoning the actions of the unfaithful partner. Instead, it is about releasing the hold that the betrayal has over your emotions and your life. It is a conscious decision to move forward, whether that means continuing the relationship or choosing to part ways. The primary goal of forgiveness is to find peace and emotional freedom, enabling you to live without the constant pain and anger associated with the betrayal.

The journey to forgiveness begins with understanding its true nature. It is not a sign of weakness or an act of submission, but rather a powerful tool for personal liberation. By forgiving, you reclaim control over your emotions and your life. This process can be incredibly empowering, as it shifts the focus from the actions of the betrayer to your own capacity for healing and growth.

Forgiveness is also a process, not a one-time event. It involves stages of grief, including denial, anger, bargaining, depression, and acceptance. You may find yourself oscillating between these stages, and that is entirely normal. The key is to allow yourself to experience these emotions fully, without rushing or forcing yourself to "get over it." Each stage has its own significance and contributes to the overall healing process.

One of the critical aspects of forgiveness is self-forgiveness. Betrayal can leave you questioning your judgment, self-worth, and actions. You might blame yourself for not seeing the signs or for contributing to the problems in the relationship. Self-forgiveness involves acknowledging that you are not responsible for your partner's actions and being kind to yourself. It means understanding that you did the best you could with the knowledge and resources you had at the time.

Practicing self-compassion is vital in the process of forgiveness. Treat yourself with the same kindness and understanding that you would offer to a friend in a similar situation. Recognize that you are human and that it is okay to feel hurt, angry, and confused. Give yourself permission to grieve the loss of trust and to heal at your own pace.

Communicating Openly and Honestly

Rebuilding trust after infidelity requires open and honest communication between partners. This communication serves as the foundation for understanding, empathy, and ultimately, forgiveness. Both partners need to be committed to transparency and to creating a safe space for expressing their feelings and concerns.

For the betrayed partner, communicating openly about the pain, anger, and confusion caused by the infidelity is crucial. This involves being honest about your emotions and expressing your needs and boundaries clearly. It is essential to communicate your expectations for the relationship moving forward and to discuss what you need from your partner to begin rebuilding trust.

On the other hand, the unfaithful partner must be willing to listen without defensiveness, acknowledge the pain they have caused, and take responsibility for their actions. This requires a high degree of humility and empathy. The betrayer must be transparent about their motivations and the circumstances that led to the infidelity. They should be prepared to answer questions and provide reassurance without becoming defensive or minimizing the betrayal.

Both partners should strive to create a safe environment for these difficult conversations. This means setting aside time to talk without distractions, practicing active listening, and being patient with each other. It is important to approach these discussions with a mindset of understanding rather than blame. The goal is to rebuild the emotional connection and establish a foundation of trust, not to rehash past arguments or assign blame.

Couples may benefit from setting ground rules for these conversations to ensure they remain constructive. This can include agreeing to take breaks if the discussion becomes too heated, avoiding name-calling or personal attacks, and staying focused on the topic at hand. It is also helpful to seek professional guidance from a therapist or counselor who can facilitate these conversations and provide tools for effective communication.

In addition to verbal communication, non-verbal communication plays a significant role in rebuilding trust. Actions often speak louder than words, and consistent, trustworthy behavior is essential for demonstrating commitment to change. This includes being reliable, keeping promises, and showing through your actions that you are dedicated to rebuilding the relationship.

Honest communication also involves setting realistic expectations. Rebuilding trust takes time, and it is important to acknowledge that there will be setbacks and challenges along the way. Both partners need to be patient and committed to the process, understanding that healing is not linear. It is normal for the betrayed partner to have lingering doubts and for the unfaithful partner to feel frustration. The key is to navigate these challenges together, with a shared goal of rebuilding trust and healing the relationship.

Forgiveness and trust are deeply intertwined. While forgiveness is a personal journey, rebuilding trust is a collaborative effort that requires mutual commitment and effort. By communicating openly and honestly, both partners can work towards understanding and healing, laying the groundwork for a renewed and stronger relationship.

In conclusion, rebuilding trust and moving towards forgiveness after infidelity is a complex and deeply personal process. It involves understanding the true nature of forgiveness, practicing self-compassion, and engaging in open and honest communication. Both partners must be committed to transparency, empathy, and consistent, trustworthy behavior. By navigating this challenging journey together, it is possible to heal from betrayal, rebuild trust, and potentially create a stronger and more resilient relationship.

Setting Boundaries and Rebuilding Trust

Setting boundaries is an essential step in the process of rebuilding trust after infidelity. Boundaries serve as a framework for what is acceptable and unacceptable in the relationship, helping both partners feel secure and respected. They create a sense of safety and predictability, which is crucial when the foundation of trust has been shaken.

The first step in setting boundaries is to engage in a candid discussion about each partner's needs and expectations. Both the betrayed and the unfaithful partner should articulate their concerns and desires clearly. For the betrayed partner, this might include needing more transparency about their partner's whereabouts, access to communication devices, or regular check-ins to rebuild a sense of security. For the unfaithful partner, it might involve understanding the betrayed partner's triggers and being mindful of behaviors that can reignite feelings of betrayal.

It is important to ensure that these boundaries are reasonable and mutually agreed upon. They should not be overly restrictive to the point of creating a surveillance-like atmosphere, as this can lead to further resentment and distrust. Instead, boundaries should aim to foster trust and open communication. Both partners need to feel comfortable and respected in these agreements, understanding that they are tools for healing rather than punitive measures.

Effective boundary-setting involves ongoing dialogue. As the relationship evolves and healing progresses, boundaries may need to be reassessed and adjusted. Regular check-ins can help both partners evaluate what is working and what might need to change. This flexibility allows the relationship to adapt and grow, preventing boundaries from becoming rigid and counterproductive.

In addition to setting boundaries, rebuilding trust requires consistent and trustworthy behavior. The unfaithful partner must demonstrate reliability and honesty in their actions. This includes keeping promises, being punctual, and following through on commitments. Trust is rebuilt through a series of consistent, positive experiences that gradually restore faith in the relationship.

Transparency is another critical component. The unfaithful partner should be open about their activities and whereabouts, voluntarily offering information to reassure the betrayed partner. This transparency is not about surveillance but about fostering an environment of openness and accountability. Over time, this openness helps to alleviate doubts and rebuild a sense of security.

It is also essential for the betrayed partner to recognize and acknowledge the unfaithful partner's efforts to rebuild trust. Positive reinforcement can be very powerful. Acknowledging small steps and improvements helps to create a positive feedback loop, encouraging further trustworthy behavior. This mutual recognition and appreciation can strengthen the emotional connection and support the healing process.

Rebuilding trust also involves addressing the root causes of the infidelity. This requires both partners to engage in self-reflection and possibly seek professional help to understand the dynamics that led to the betrayal. It might involve exploring issues related to communication, unmet needs, or underlying personal struggles. By addressing these root causes, both partners can work towards preventing future betrayals and building a healthier, more resilient relationship.

Forgiveness and trust are not linear processes, and setbacks are inevitable. There will be moments of doubt, fear, and anger. Both partners must be prepared for these challenges and committed to working through them together. Patience, empathy, and a willingness to forgive oneself and each other are essential.

For the unfaithful partner, it is important to understand that regaining trust will take time and that the betrayed partner's healing process cannot be rushed. They must be prepared to offer continued reassurance and support, even when it feels frustrating or repetitive. Demonstrating patience and understanding can help to rebuild trust incrementally.

For the betrayed partner, it is important to practice self-compassion and recognize that rebuilding trust is a gradual process. There will be days when it feels like progress is being made and days when the pain feels overwhelming. Allowing oneself to experience and express these emotions without judgment is crucial for healing.

In some cases, the process of rebuilding trust might reveal that the relationship is no longer viable. This realization can be painful, but it is important to acknowledge it honestly. If the relationship cannot be rebuilt, both partners must allow themselves the grace to move on and seek healing individually. Ending the relationship does not signify failure but rather an acknowledgment of what is best for each person's well-being.

Rebuilding trust after infidelity is one of the most challenging journeys a couple can undertake, but it is possible with commitment, empathy, and hard work. By setting clear boundaries, communicating openly, and demonstrating consistent, trustworthy behavior, both partners can work towards healing and rebuilding their relationship. This process requires time, patience, and a willingness to confront and address deep emotional wounds. However, through this challenging journey, couples can emerge stronger, with a deeper understanding of themselves and each other, and with the possibility of a renewed and more resilient relationship.

CHAPTER 5

Self-Care and Personal Growth

Importance of Self-Care

In the aftermath of infidelity, self-care becomes a vital component of the healing journey. The emotional upheaval caused by betrayal can be all-consuming, making it easy to neglect personal well-being. However, prioritizing self-care is crucial not only for managing the immediate emotional impact but also for fostering long-term recovery and personal growth. Self-care encompasses a range of practices that support physical, emotional, and mental well-being, and it plays a central role in helping individuals regain their sense of balance and control.

Self-care is more than just occasional indulgence; it is a consistent practice that involves making deliberate choices to support your overall health. After infidelity, it is common to experience a wide range of emotions, including anger, sadness, and confusion. Engaging in self-care helps to manage these emotions and provides a foundation for emotional stability. This is particularly important when navigating the complex feelings that arise from betrayal, as they can be overwhelming and exhausting.

Physical self-care is one of the most immediate ways to support your well-being. When dealing with stress and emotional turmoil, it is easy to overlook basic needs such as proper nutrition, exercise, and adequate rest. Yet, these elements are essential for maintaining physical health and supporting emotional resilience. Regular physical activity, such as walking, yoga, or exercise classes, can help reduce stress, improve mood, and enhance overall well-being. Eating a balanced diet and ensuring sufficient sleep are equally important, as they provide the energy and physical support needed to cope with emotional challenges.

Emotional self-care involves acknowledging and addressing your feelings in a healthy and constructive manner. This might include practices such as journaling, meditation, or engaging in hobbies that bring joy and relaxation. Journaling can be particularly therapeutic, as it allows you to process and articulate your emotions in a private and safe space. Meditation and mindfulness practices can help calm the mind and reduce the intensity of negative emotions, fostering a sense of inner peace and clarity.

Engaging in activities that bring pleasure and fulfillment is also an essential aspect of emotional self-care. Pursuing hobbies, spending time with supportive friends, or engaging in creative outlets can provide a much-needed distraction and boost your mood. These activities help to reinforce a sense of identity and purpose beyond the immediate pain of betrayal, contributing to overall emotional well-being.

Mental self-care is equally important and involves fostering a positive mindset and addressing any negative thought patterns. Infidelity can lead to self-doubt and a diminished sense of self-worth. Practicing self-compassion and challenging negative self-talk are crucial for rebuilding confidence and maintaining a healthy self-image. Cognitive-behavioral techniques, such as identifying and reframing negative thoughts, can be effective in promoting a more positive outlook and reducing anxiety and depression.

Setting boundaries and learning to say no are also vital components of self-care. In the aftermath of infidelity, it is important to protect your emotional space and avoid situations or interactions that exacerbate stress or discomfort. This might involve limiting contact with individuals who are not supportive, declining invitations or activities that feel overwhelming, and prioritizing time for yourself. Establishing and maintaining boundaries helps to create a safe and nurturing environment in which you can focus on healing and personal growth.

Self-care also involves seeking professional support when needed. Therapy or counseling can provide a valuable space for exploring your emotions, gaining insight, and developing coping strategies. A mental health professional can offer guidance and support tailored to your specific needs, helping you navigate the complexities of recovery and personal growth. Therapy can also assist in identifying and addressing underlying issues that may have contributed to the infidelity, facilitating a more comprehensive healing process.

Personal growth is a natural and important aspect of the self-care journey. Infidelity often prompts individuals to reevaluate their values, goals, and relationships. This period of reflection can be an opportunity for significant personal development and self-discovery. By engaging in self-care practices, you create the space and energy needed to explore new interests, set new goals, and build a stronger sense of self.

One of the key aspects of personal growth is developing resilience. Resilience is the ability to adapt and thrive despite adversity, and it is a crucial skill for navigating the challenges of healing after betrayal. Building resilience involves cultivating a positive mindset, learning from setbacks, and maintaining hope for the future. Engaging in self-care practices strengthens your resilience by providing the support and resources needed to cope with stress and adversity.

Another important aspect of personal growth is learning to embrace change and uncertainty. Infidelity often brings significant changes to your life and relationship, and adapting to these changes can be challenging. By focusing on self-care and personal growth, you can develop a greater sense of flexibility and adaptability. Embracing change as an opportunity for growth can help you navigate the uncertainties of recovery and build a more fulfilling and resilient life.

Self-care and personal growth are intertwined, and investing in one supports the other. By prioritizing your well-being and engaging in practices that foster emotional, physical, and mental health, you create a strong foundation for personal growth and healing. This holistic approach to self-care enables you to rebuild your sense of self, gain clarity, and move forward with confidence and resilience.

Self-care is a fundamental component of healing and personal growth after infidelity. It involves prioritizing your physical, emotional, and mental well-being through consistent and intentional practices. By engaging in self-care, you support your overall health, manage emotional challenges, and foster resilience. Personal growth emerges from this process, providing an opportunity for self-discovery, adaptation, and positive change. Investing in self-care and personal growth not only aids in recovery but also paves the way for a more fulfilling and empowered future.

Activities for Mental and Emotional Well-being

Engaging in activities that promote mental and emotional well-being is crucial for recovery and personal growth following infidelity. These activities help manage stress, foster emotional balance, and rebuild a sense of self-worth. Incorporating a variety of practices into your daily routine can provide a holistic approach to healing and contribute to overall well-being.

One effective activity for enhancing mental and emotional health is mindfulness and meditation. These practices involve focusing your attention on the present moment and cultivating an attitude of acceptance and non-judgment. Mindfulness techniques, such as mindful breathing and body scans, can help calm the mind, reduce anxiety, and promote a greater sense of inner peace. Meditation, even if practiced for just a few minutes each day, can help shift your perspective, enhance emotional resilience, and improve overall mental clarity.

Another valuable activity is journaling. Writing about your thoughts and feelings provides an opportunity to process and articulate emotions that may be difficult to express verbally. Journaling can be a therapeutic outlet for exploring your inner world, tracking your progress, and gaining insight into your healing journey. It also allows you to reflect on your experiences, set goals, and celebrate achievements, reinforcing a sense of growth and accomplishment.

Engaging in regular physical exercise is also beneficial for mental and emotional well-being. Physical activity releases endorphins, which are natural mood lifters, and helps reduce the symptoms of anxiety and depression. Activities such as walking, running, swimming, or participating in fitness classes can enhance your overall mood, increase energy levels, and promote a sense of achievement. Exercise also provides a constructive outlet for stress and helps improve sleep quality, further supporting emotional health.

Creative pursuits, such as art, music, or writing, offer additional avenues for emotional expression and healing. Engaging in creative activities allows you to channel your emotions into something productive and meaningful. Art therapy, for example, can help you explore and express complex feelings through visual media. Music therapy, whether through listening, playing an instrument, or singing, can evoke and release emotions, providing comfort and solace. Creative writing, including poetry or fiction, can offer a space for self-expression and exploration of personal experiences.

Building and maintaining social connections is another key aspect of mental and emotional well-being. Positive social interactions provide support, encouragement, and a sense of belonging. Spending time with friends and family, participating in social activities, and nurturing relationships can offer comfort and reduce feelings of isolation. It is important to surround yourself with individuals who are empathetic and supportive, as their presence can significantly impact your healing process.

Self-care practices, such as engaging in relaxation techniques, are also important for managing stress and promoting emotional balance. Techniques such as deep breathing exercises, progressive muscle relaxation, and guided imagery can help calm the nervous system and reduce stress levels. Incorporating these practices into your daily routine can enhance your overall sense of well-being and provide a sense of control over your emotional state.

Pursuing Hobbies and Interests

Pursuing hobbies and interests plays a vital role in the healing process and personal growth following infidelity. Hobbies and interests provide a sense of purpose, joy, and fulfillment, helping to rebuild a positive sense of self and redirect focus away from the pain of betrayal. Engaging in activities that you are passionate about or exploring new interests can significantly contribute to emotional and mental well-being.

Hobbies offer a valuable distraction from distressing thoughts and emotions. By immersing yourself in activities that you enjoy, you create opportunities for relaxation and positive engagement. This can help shift your focus away from the trauma of infidelity and foster a sense of accomplishment and satisfaction. Whether it is gardening, painting, cooking, or playing a musical instrument, engaging in hobbies allows you to experience pleasure and fulfillment, reinforcing a positive outlook and enhancing overall well-being.

Exploring new interests and activities can also be a powerful tool for personal growth. Trying something new can open up opportunities for self-discovery, build confidence, and introduce you to new social circles. It provides a chance to expand your horizons, develop new skills, and embrace change. Engaging in new experiences can help you rediscover your passions and interests, fostering a renewed sense of identity and purpose.

Participating in hobbies and interests can also facilitate social connections. Many hobbies offer opportunities to meet like-minded individuals and build supportive relationships. Joining clubs, classes, or groups related to your interests can help you connect with others who share similar passions. These social interactions can provide valuable support, encouragement, and a sense of community, contributing to your emotional healing and growth.

Additionally, pursuing hobbies can enhance your sense of accomplishment and self-worth. Setting and achieving goals related to your hobbies, such as completing a project or mastering a new skill, can boost your confidence and reinforce a positive self-image. This sense of achievement contributes to a greater overall sense of well-being and satisfaction, helping you build resilience and confidence in your ability to overcome challenges.

Engaging in hobbies and interests also encourages a balanced lifestyle. By incorporating activities that bring joy and fulfillment into your routine, you create a more balanced approach to life. This balance helps mitigate the effects of stress and emotional upheaval, contributing to a healthier and more harmonious state of being.

In summary, activities for mental and emotional well-being, as well as pursuing hobbies and interests, play crucial roles in the recovery and personal growth process after infidelity. Mindfulness, journaling, exercise, creative pursuits, and social connections offer valuable support for emotional healing and resilience. Additionally, engaging in hobbies and exploring new interests provide opportunities for joy, self-discovery, and a renewed sense of purpose. By integrating these practices into your life, you create a foundation for healing, growth, and a more fulfilling future.

Part III

Long-Term Recovery and Growth

CHAPTER 6

Navigating Relationship Dynamics Post-Infidelity

In the wake of infidelity, reassessing relationship goals becomes a crucial step in the healing and recovery process. Infidelity fundamentally alters the dynamics of a relationship, often prompting both partners to reevaluate their expectations, desires, and long-term objectives. This reassessment is essential for rebuilding a healthier, more resilient partnership, or in some cases, deciding to part ways with clarity and mutual respect.

Reassessing Relationship Goals

The initial discovery of infidelity brings about a crisis that disrupts the established trust and stability within a relationship. In the aftermath, both partners may feel a range of intense emotions, including betrayal, anger, sadness, and confusion. Amidst this emotional turmoil, it is important to pause and reflect on the future of the relationship. This period of reflection is an opportunity to examine the underlying issues that led to the infidelity and to determine whether the relationship can be repaired and how it might be redefined.

Reassessing relationship goals involves an honest and open dialogue between partners. This conversation requires a safe and non-judgmental environment where both individuals can express their thoughts and feelings freely. It is essential to communicate openly about what each partner wants from the relationship moving forward. These discussions should address fundamental questions such as: What are our individual and shared values? What are our long-term aspirations? What do we need from each other to feel secure and fulfilled in this relationship?

One of the first steps in this reassessment process is to evaluate the relationship's core foundation. Trust, respect, and communication are the cornerstones of any healthy partnership. Infidelity severely damages trust, and rebuilding it requires a concerted effort from both partners. The unfaithful partner must demonstrate genuine remorse, transparency, and a commitment to change. Meanwhile, the betrayed partner needs to assess their capacity to forgive and rebuild trust. This process is neither quick nor easy, but with dedication and mutual effort, it is possible to restore a sense of trust and security.

Respect is another critical component that needs reassessment. Infidelity often leaves the betrayed partner feeling devalued and disrespected. Reestablishing mutual respect involves acknowledging the hurt caused and committing to treat each other with kindness and consideration. Both partners need to feel heard, valued, and understood in their interactions. This respect is demonstrated through consistent, caring behavior and a willingness to prioritize each other's well-being.

Communication is the lifeline of a relationship, and after infidelity, it becomes even more crucial. Effective communication involves not only speaking openly but also listening actively. Partners need to develop skills to express their needs, fears, and hopes clearly and constructively. This includes being honest about the impact of the infidelity and discussing how to prevent future breaches of trust. Regular, honest communication helps to clear misunderstandings and fosters a deeper connection.

As part of reassessing relationship goals, it is important to explore the reasons behind the infidelity. Understanding the factors that contributed to the betrayal can provide valuable insights into the relationship's dynamics and areas that need improvement. These factors can range from unmet emotional needs, lack of intimacy, or personal issues that one or both partners may be facing. By identifying and addressing these root causes, couples can work towards creating a more fulfilling and supportive relationship.

Setting new relationship goals involves creating a shared vision for the future. This vision should encompass both individual aspirations and collective objectives. It is important to discuss and align on aspects such as career goals, family planning, financial priorities, and personal growth. This alignment helps to ensure that both partners are working towards common goals and supporting each other's individual dreams.

Rebuilding intimacy is another significant aspect of reassessing relationship goals. Infidelity often creates a rift in emotional and physical intimacy. Reconnecting on an emotional level involves spending quality time together, sharing experiences, and nurturing a deep sense of closeness. Physical intimacy, which might be strained after infidelity, needs to be rebuilt gradually and respectfully, ensuring that both partners feel comfortable and valued.

Boundaries play a critical role in this reassessment process. Setting clear and healthy boundaries helps to protect the relationship from future breaches of trust. These boundaries should be mutually agreed upon and respected by both partners. They might include guidelines about communication with ex-partners, transparency in digital communications, or agreed-upon behaviors that promote trust and respect.

Forgiveness is a complex but essential part of moving forward. It involves letting go of the anger and resentment associated with the betrayal. Forgiveness does not mean forgetting or condoning the infidelity; rather, it is about freeing oneself from the burden of negative emotions and making a conscious choice to work towards healing. Both partners must engage in this process, with the unfaithful partner demonstrating genuine remorse and the betrayed partner finding a path to release their hurt.

Therapy can be an invaluable tool during this period of reassessment. A skilled therapist can provide a neutral space for both partners to explore their feelings, communicate effectively, and develop strategies for rebuilding their relationship. Therapy can also help individuals work through their personal issues and trauma related to the infidelity, promoting overall emotional health.

Ultimately, reassessing relationship goals is about creating a new, stronger foundation. It involves acknowledging the past, learning from it, and committing to a future built on mutual trust, respect, and understanding. This process requires time, patience, and a willingness to embrace vulnerability. By engaging in honest dialogue, setting shared goals, and working together to rebuild trust, couples can navigate the complexities of post-infidelity dynamics and emerge with a renewed and more resilient relationship.

Navigating relationship dynamics post-infidelity requires a thorough reassessment of relationship goals. This involves open communication, rebuilding trust and respect, understanding the root causes of infidelity, setting new goals, and fostering emotional and physical intimacy. With dedication and mutual effort, couples can redefine their relationship and build a stronger, healthier partnership.

Techniques for Effective Communication

Effective communication is the backbone of any healthy relationship, and it becomes even more crucial after experiencing infidelity. Rebuilding trust and fostering a deeper connection requires both partners to engage in honest, respectful, and constructive dialogue. Developing strong communication skills can help couples navigate their emotions, address underlying issues, and establish a new foundation for their relationship.

One of the most important techniques for effective communication is active listening. Active listening involves fully concentrating on what the other person is saying without interrupting or planning your response while they are speaking. It requires being present in the moment, showing empathy, and validating your partner's feelings. This practice helps to ensure that both partners feel heard and understood, which is essential for rebuilding trust and intimacy. To enhance active listening, use nonverbal cues such as nodding, maintaining eye contact, and providing feedback like summarizing or paraphrasing what your partner has said.

Using "I" statements instead of "you" statements can significantly improve communication by reducing defensiveness and promoting a more collaborative conversation. For example, saying "I feel hurt when I think about what happened" is more effective than saying "You hurt me when you cheated." "I" statements focus on your own feelings and experiences, making it easier for your partner to understand your perspective without feeling attacked.

Another technique is to practice empathy and validation. Empathy involves putting yourself in your partner's shoes and trying to understand their feelings and experiences. Validation means acknowledging and accepting your partner's emotions, even if you do not necessarily agree with their point of view. Validating your partner's feelings shows that you respect their emotions and are willing to support them through the healing process. Phrases like "I understand that you're feeling..." or "It makes sense that you would feel..." can be very helpful.

Setting aside regular time for open and honest conversations can also enhance communication. Designate a specific time each week to discuss your relationship, share your thoughts and feelings, and address any concerns. This practice ensures that communication remains a priority and provides a safe space for both partners to express themselves without distractions.

Nonverbal communication is just as important as verbal communication. Pay attention to your body language, facial expressions, and tone of voice, as these can convey emotions and intentions more powerfully than words alone. Ensure that your nonverbal cues align with your verbal messages to avoid misunderstandings and to convey sincerity and openness.

Being mindful of timing and context is another crucial aspect of effective communication. Choose an appropriate time and place for serious discussions, ensuring that both partners are in a calm and receptive state of mind. Avoid starting difficult conversations when either partner is tired, stressed, or distracted, as this can lead to heightened emotions and ineffective communication.

Practicing patience and taking breaks during heated discussions can prevent conversations from escalating into arguments. If emotions start to run high, it can be helpful to take a short break to cool down and collect your thoughts. Agreeing on a signal or phrase to indicate the need for a break can help manage these situations constructively. During the break, engage in calming activities such as deep breathing, walking, or listening to soothing music before resuming the conversation.

Managing Conflicts Constructively

Conflict is a natural part of any relationship, but managing it constructively is essential for maintaining a healthy and supportive partnership. After infidelity, conflicts may become more frequent and intense due to heightened emotions and mistrust. Learning how to manage these conflicts effectively can help to prevent further damage and promote healing.

One key strategy for managing conflicts constructively is to stay focused on the issue at hand. Avoid bringing up past grievances or unrelated problems during a conflict. Concentrate on the specific issue that needs to be addressed and work together to find a resolution. This approach helps to prevent conflicts from becoming overwhelming and keeps the discussion productive.

Using a problem-solving approach can be very effective in managing conflicts. Identify the issue clearly, brainstorm possible solutions, and evaluate the pros and cons of each option together. Collaboratively selecting a solution that both partners can agree on fosters a sense of teamwork and mutual respect. This method emphasizes finding a resolution rather than placing blame.

Maintaining respect and avoiding hurtful language during conflicts is crucial. Name-calling, insults, and other forms of disrespect can cause deep emotional wounds and erode trust further. Focus on expressing your feelings and needs without attacking your partner. Phrases like "I feel..." or "I need..." can help to communicate your perspective without being confrontational.

Recognizing and acknowledging your own role in the conflict is also important. Take responsibility for your actions and be willing to apologize if necessary. Owning your part in the issue demonstrates accountability and a commitment to improving the relationship. It also encourages your partner to do the same, fostering a more collaborative and respectful dynamic.

Another effective technique for managing conflicts is to practice compromise and flexibility. Be willing to meet your partner halfway and find solutions that satisfy both parties. Compromise does not mean giving up your needs or values but finding a balance that works for both partners. Flexibility allows for creative problem-solving and demonstrates a willingness to prioritize the relationship.

Creating and enforcing boundaries is an essential aspect of conflict management. Clear boundaries help to establish guidelines for acceptable behavior and interactions, preventing conflicts from escalating into hurtful exchanges. Discuss and agree on boundaries together, ensuring that both partners feel comfortable and respected. Enforcing these boundaries consistently helps to maintain a safe and supportive environment for resolving conflicts.

Seeking external support when necessary can also be beneficial. Couples therapy or counseling can provide a neutral space for addressing conflicts and improving communication skills. A trained therapist can offer valuable insights, tools, and techniques for managing conflicts constructively and fostering a healthier relationship dynamic.

In conclusion, navigating relationship dynamics post-infidelity requires a commitment to effective communication and constructive conflict management. By developing strong communication skills such as active listening, using "I" statements, practicing empathy, and setting regular times for open conversations, couples can rebuild trust and foster a deeper connection. Managing conflicts constructively through problem-solving, maintaining respect, recognizing personal accountability, and seeking compromise helps to prevent further damage and promote healing. With dedication and mutual effort, couples can redefine their relationship and build a stronger, more resilient partnership.

CHAPTER 7

Healing as a Couple

Healing from infidelity is an arduous journey that often requires the guidance and support of professionals. Joint therapy and counseling can play a pivotal role in helping couples navigate the complex emotions and challenges that arise after betrayal. By providing a safe and structured environment for communication, joint therapy facilitates understanding, fosters empathy, and promotes healing on both an individual and relational level.

Joint Therapy and Counseling

Joint therapy, also known as couples therapy, is a form of psychotherapy that focuses on improving relationship dynamics and resolving conflicts between partners. This therapeutic approach is particularly beneficial after infidelity, as it addresses the breach of trust and its impact on the relationship. A trained therapist acts as a mediator, helping couples to communicate more effectively, understand each other's perspectives, and develop strategies for rebuilding trust.

One of the primary benefits of joint therapy is that it provides a neutral space where both partners can express their thoughts and feelings openly. In the aftermath of infidelity, emotions can run high, making it difficult for couples to communicate constructively. A therapist can facilitate these conversations, ensuring that both partners feel heard and validated. This open dialogue is crucial for addressing the pain and confusion caused by infidelity and for laying the groundwork for healing.

Joint therapy also helps couples to explore the underlying issues that contributed to the infidelity. While the act of cheating is never justified, understanding the factors that led to the betrayal can provide valuable insights into the relationship's weaknesses. These factors may include unmet emotional needs, communication breakdowns, or individual psychological issues. By identifying and addressing these root causes, couples can work towards creating a more fulfilling and resilient relationship.

Another important aspect of joint therapy is rebuilding trust. Trust is the foundation of any healthy relationship, and infidelity shatters this trust, leaving both partners feeling vulnerable and insecure. Rebuilding trust requires a commitment to transparency, honesty, and consistent behavior over time. In therapy, couples can learn techniques for rebuilding trust, such as establishing open communication channels, setting boundaries, and creating accountability. A therapist can guide this process, providing support and strategies to help both partners feel more secure.

Joint therapy also emphasizes the importance of empathy and understanding. Infidelity often leaves the betrayed partner feeling deeply hurt and betrayed, while the unfaithful partner may experience guilt and shame. Through therapy, both partners can learn to empathize with each other's experiences and emotions. This empathy fosters a deeper connection and mutual support, which are essential for healing. By understanding each other's pain, couples can begin to move forward together, rather than being stuck in a cycle of blame and resentment.

Conflict resolution is another critical component of joint therapy. After infidelity, conflicts may become more frequent and intense due to heightened emotions and mistrust. A therapist can teach couples effective conflict resolution techniques, such as active listening, using "I" statements, and practicing empathy. These skills help couples to navigate disagreements constructively, preventing conflicts from escalating and causing further harm. Learning to manage conflicts in a healthy way is essential for maintaining a supportive and loving relationship.

Joint therapy also provides an opportunity for couples to redefine their relationship goals. Infidelity often prompts a reassessment of what each partner wants from the relationship and how they envision their future together. Through therapy, couples can explore their individual and shared goals, values, and aspirations. This process helps to create a shared vision for the future, ensuring that both partners are aligned and committed to the same objectives. By setting new goals and working towards them together, couples can strengthen their bond and build a more resilient partnership.

In addition to addressing the immediate aftermath of infidelity, joint therapy can also promote long-term personal and relational growth. Therapy provides a space for both partners to explore their individual issues and work on personal development. This personal growth can enhance the relationship, as both partners become more self-aware and emotionally healthy. By investing in their own well-being, couples can create a stronger and more supportive partnership.

Joint therapy can also include elements of individual therapy, where each partner works on their personal issues with the guidance of the same or different therapist. This combined approach ensures that both individual and relational issues are addressed, promoting comprehensive healing. Individual therapy can help each partner to process their emotions, develop coping strategies, and work through any personal trauma or psychological issues that may have contributed to the infidelity.

Another benefit of joint therapy is that it provides a structured approach to healing. The therapeutic process typically involves setting goals, developing strategies, and monitoring progress. This structured approach helps to ensure that both partners are actively engaged in the healing process and making tangible progress. A therapist can provide regular feedback and adjustments to the therapy plan, ensuring that it meets the evolving needs of the couple.

It is important to note that joint therapy is not a quick fix. Healing from infidelity takes time, effort, and commitment from both partners. The therapy process may involve difficult conversations, emotional pain, and setbacks. However, with the guidance of a skilled therapist and a willingness to work together, couples can navigate these challenges and emerge stronger.

Joint therapy and counseling are invaluable tools for couples seeking to heal from infidelity. By providing a safe and structured environment for communication, therapy helps couples to understand each other's perspectives, rebuild trust, and address the underlying issues that led to the betrayal. Through empathy, effective conflict resolution, and a commitment to personal and relational growth, couples can navigate the complex emotions and challenges of infidelity and build a stronger, more resilient partnership. While the journey of healing is not easy, joint therapy offers hope and guidance for couples committed to rebuilding their relationship and moving forward together.

Re-establishing Intimacy

Re-establishing intimacy after infidelity is one of the most challenging yet crucial steps in the healing process. Intimacy, both emotional and physical, forms the cornerstone of a healthy relationship. Infidelity often creates a significant rift in this intimacy, leaving both partners feeling disconnected and vulnerable. The journey to rekindle this closeness requires patience, understanding, and a mutual commitment to rebuilding the bond.

Emotional intimacy is the first area that needs attention. Emotional intimacy involves a deep connection where partners feel understood, supported, and valued. After infidelity, emotional intimacy is often shattered, as trust has been broken and feelings of betrayal dominate. Rebuilding this connection starts with open, honest communication. Both partners need to express their feelings, fears, and hopes without judgment. This transparency fosters a sense of safety and understanding, allowing for emotional reconnection.

Practicing empathy plays a vital role in re-establishing emotional intimacy. Both partners must strive to understand each other's experiences and emotions. The betrayed partner may feel immense pain and distrust, while the unfaithful partner may experience guilt and shame. Empathizing with these feelings helps to validate each other's emotions and paves the way for deeper emotional connection. This empathy can be nurtured through regular, heartfelt conversations where each partner listens actively and responds with compassion.

Quality time is another essential component in rebuilding emotional intimacy. Spending time together without distractions helps to strengthen the bond between partners. Engaging in activities that both enjoy, such as cooking, walking, or watching movies, can create positive shared experiences. These moments help to rebuild trust and remind both partners of the connection they once had.

Physical intimacy, often affected by infidelity, also needs careful rebuilding. Physical touch, such as holding hands, hugging, and kissing, is crucial for maintaining a connection. However, the pace at which physical intimacy is reintroduced should be comfortable for both partners. It's important to communicate openly about physical boundaries and respect each other's comfort levels. Gradually reintroducing physical affection can help both partners feel more connected and secure.

Sexual intimacy, a sensitive area post-infidelity, requires time and patience. Trust and emotional safety are prerequisites for a healthy sexual relationship. Partners should discuss their feelings and anxieties openly and decide together when they feel ready to resume sexual activity. It's essential to approach this aspect of the relationship with empathy and understanding, ensuring that both partners feel valued and respected.

Therapy can be incredibly beneficial in this aspect. A therapist can guide couples through the process of re-establishing both emotional and physical intimacy. They can provide strategies for rebuilding trust, enhancing communication, and reconnecting on a deeper level. Through therapy, couples can explore their intimacy issues in a safe and supportive environment, learning to navigate the complexities of their renewed relationship.

Setting New Relationship Norms

Setting new relationship norms is an integral part of rebuilding a relationship after infidelity. Infidelity often reveals underlying issues and dysfunctional patterns within the relationship. Addressing these issues and establishing new, healthier norms is crucial for preventing future problems and fostering a more resilient partnership.

One of the first steps in setting new norms is to define clear boundaries. Boundaries are essential for maintaining trust and respect in a relationship. Partners need to discuss and agree on what behaviors are acceptable and what are not. This could include guidelines around communication with ex-partners, transparency with digital devices, and expectations around time spent together. Setting and respecting these boundaries help to create a sense of security and trust.

Establishing new communication norms is also vital. Effective communication involves more than just talking; it requires active listening, empathy, and honesty. Partners should commit to regular, open dialogues where they can discuss their feelings, needs, and concerns without fear of judgment. These conversations help to address issues before they escalate and ensure that both partners feel heard and valued.

Trust-building practices should be an integral part of the new relationship norms. Trust is the foundation of any healthy relationship, and rebuilding it requires consistent effort and transparency. Partners can establish practices such as regular check-ins, sharing daily experiences, and being open about their activities and whereabouts. These practices foster transparency and demonstrate a commitment to honesty and integrity.

Mutual respect is another critical norm that needs to be reinforced. Infidelity often leaves the betrayed partner feeling disrespected and devalued. Re-establishing respect involves treating each other with kindness, consideration, and appreciation. This includes acknowledging each other's contributions, supporting each other's goals, and addressing conflicts respectfully. Consistently demonstrating respect helps to rebuild the emotional foundation of the relationship.

Another important norm is prioritizing the relationship. In the aftermath of infidelity, it's essential to make the relationship a top priority. This involves dedicating time and effort to nurturing the connection, whether through date nights, shared hobbies, or simply spending quality time together. Prioritizing the relationship helps to strengthen the bond and create a sense of unity and partnership.

Self-care should also be incorporated into the new relationship norms. Both partners need to prioritize their own well-being and personal growth. This could involve pursuing hobbies, engaging in physical activities, or seeking individual therapy. By taking care of themselves, partners can bring their best selves to the relationship, contributing to a healthier dynamic.

Conflict resolution is another area where new norms are essential. Conflicts are inevitable in any relationship, but how they are managed makes a significant difference. Partners should commit to addressing conflicts constructively, using techniques such as active listening, empathy, and compromise. Avoiding blame and focusing on finding solutions together helps to prevent conflicts from causing further damage.

Joint goal-setting can also be a valuable new norm. Setting shared goals helps to align both partners towards a common vision for the future. These goals can be related to various aspects of life, such as financial planning, career aspirations, or family planning. Working towards shared goals fosters a sense of teamwork and mutual support, strengthening the relationship.

Celebrating progress and achievements is another positive norm. Recognizing and celebrating each other's efforts and milestones, whether big or small, helps to create a positive and encouraging atmosphere. This could involve acknowledging personal achievements, celebrating anniversaries, or simply expressing gratitude for each other's presence and contributions. Celebrating progress reinforces positive behavior and encourages continued growth.

In conclusion, re-establishing intimacy and setting new relationship norms are crucial steps in the healing journey after infidelity. By focusing on rebuilding emotional and physical intimacy through open communication, empathy, and quality time, couples can reconnect and strengthen their bond. Establishing new norms around boundaries, communication, trust, respect, and conflict resolution helps to create a healthier and more resilient partnership. Through mutual effort, dedication, and support, couples can navigate the complexities of healing and build a stronger, more fulfilling relationship.

CHAPTER 8

Moving Forward: Building a New Future

Moving forward after infidelity is a challenging but transformative process that involves embracing change and fostering personal growth. Infidelity can be a devastating blow to any relationship, but it also presents an opportunity for profound personal and relational transformation. Embracing change means letting go of past hurts and adopting new perspectives, while personal growth involves becoming the best version of oneself for the benefit of both the individual and the relationship.

Embracing Change and Personal Growth

Embracing change begins with accepting the reality of the situation. Infidelity fundamentally alters the dynamics of a relationship, and both partners must acknowledge that the relationship will never be the same as it was before. This acceptance is not about resigning to a lesser relationship, but rather recognizing that a new chapter must begin.

Acceptance allows both partners to release the hold of past grievances and opens the door to building a healthier, more resilient relationship.

One of the first steps in embracing change is cultivating a mindset of forgiveness. Forgiveness is a complex and deeply personal process that involves letting go of resentment and anger. It does not mean condoning the betrayal or forgetting the pain it caused, but rather choosing to release the hold that these negative emotions have on one's life. Forgiveness is crucial for personal peace and the health of the relationship. It allows both partners to move forward without the burden of past hurts weighing them down.

Another essential aspect of embracing change is fostering open and honest communication. The aftermath of infidelity often leaves both partners feeling disconnected and uncertain. Rebuilding communication channels helps to bridge this gap and create a foundation of trust and transparency. Honest conversations about feelings, expectations, and future goals are necessary to align both partners and ensure that they are working towards a common vision. This open dialogue also helps to prevent misunderstandings and allows for the continuous adjustment of relationship dynamics as both partners grow and change.

Personal growth is equally important in the journey of moving forward. Infidelity often exposes underlying issues within the relationship and within each individual. Addressing these issues through personal development can lead to a more fulfilling and balanced life. Personal growth involves self-reflection, understanding one's strengths and weaknesses, and making conscious efforts to improve. This journey can include pursuing new interests, developing new skills, or addressing personal shortcomings that may have contributed to relationship problems.

Self-care is a critical component of personal growth. After experiencing the emotional turmoil of infidelity, it is essential for both partners to prioritize their physical, emotional, and mental well-being. Self-care practices such as regular exercise, meditation, journaling, and engaging in hobbies can significantly improve overall well-being. Taking time for oneself helps to recharge and provides the emotional strength needed to navigate the complexities of rebuilding a relationship. When individuals take care of themselves, they are better equipped to support their partners and contribute positively to the relationship.

Therapy and counseling can play a significant role in personal growth and embracing change. Individual therapy allows each partner to explore their emotions, understand their behavior patterns, and develop healthy coping mechanisms. It provides a safe space to process the pain and trauma caused by infidelity and to work through any personal issues that may have been exposed. Through therapy, individuals can gain insights into their emotional triggers and learn strategies to manage them effectively.

Joint therapy, or couples therapy, further supports this growth by addressing relational dynamics and fostering a collaborative approach to healing. In joint therapy, couples learn how to communicate more effectively, resolve conflicts constructively, and rebuild trust. The therapist acts as a guide, helping couples to navigate their emotions and develop a deeper understanding of each other. This process not only heals the wounds caused by infidelity but also strengthens the relationship, making it more resilient to future challenges.

Embracing change also involves setting new goals and aspirations for the relationship. Infidelity often serves as a wake-up call, prompting couples to re-evaluate their relationship priorities and future plans. Setting new goals together helps to create a sense of purpose and direction. These goals can include improving communication, spending more quality time together, pursuing joint interests, or even making significant life changes such as moving to a new place or starting a family. By working towards common goals, couples can foster a sense of unity and shared purpose, which strengthens their bond.

Re-establishing intimacy is another critical aspect of moving forward. Infidelity often damages the emotional and physical intimacy between partners. Rebuilding this intimacy requires patience, effort, and a willingness to be vulnerable. Emotional intimacy can be nurtured through open conversations, empathy, and spending quality time together. Physical intimacy, which may take longer to re-establish, should be approached with sensitivity and respect for each other's boundaries. Gradually rebuilding these aspects of intimacy helps to restore the connection and trust that are essential for a healthy relationship.

Lastly, embracing change and personal growth involves adopting a mindset of continuous improvement. Relationships, like individuals, are constantly evolving. Committing to ongoing growth and improvement ensures that both partners remain engaged and invested in the relationship. This commitment can be manifested through regular check-ins, seeking new experiences together, and continuously working on communication and conflict resolution skills. By embracing this mindset, couples can create a dynamic and resilient relationship that can withstand the challenges of life.

Moving forward after infidelity requires embracing change and fostering personal growth. Accepting the reality of the situation, cultivating forgiveness, and fostering open communication are essential steps in this journey. Personal growth through self-care, therapy, and setting new goals helps to address underlying issues and build a stronger foundation. Re-establishing intimacy and adopting a mindset of continuous improvement further support the healing process. While the journey is undoubtedly challenging, embracing change and committing to personal growth can lead to a more fulfilling and resilient relationship, where both partners can thrive and build a new future together.

Setting Future Goals as an Individual and as a Couple

Setting future goals, both individually and as a couple, is a vital part of moving forward after infidelity. These goals provide direction and a sense of purpose, helping to guide the relationship towards a healthier, more fulfilling future. They also foster a sense of unity and shared vision, which is crucial for rebuilding trust and intimacy.

Individual goals are essential for personal growth and self-fulfillment. After the upheaval caused by infidelity, focusing on personal development can help individuals regain a sense of control and confidence. These goals might include pursuing further education, advancing in a career, developing new skills, or improving physical health. Setting and working towards these goals allows individuals to invest in themselves, building self-esteem and resilience. It also ensures that they bring their best selves to the relationship, contributing positively to its growth.

Individual goals should also encompass emotional and psychological well-being. This might involve engaging in regular therapy or counseling, practicing mindfulness and meditation, or participating in activities that promote emotional health. By prioritizing their well-being, individuals can better manage the stresses and challenges of life and relationships, creating a more stable and supportive partnership.

As a couple, setting joint goals is equally important. These goals create a shared vision for the future, aligning both partners towards common objectives and reinforcing their commitment to each other. Joint goals can vary widely, from improving communication skills and spending more quality time together, to significant life decisions such as buying a home, traveling, or starting a family.

One crucial area for joint goal-setting is improving communication. Effective communication is the foundation of a healthy relationship, especially after infidelity. Couples can set goals to engage in regular, honest dialogues, perhaps by scheduling weekly check-ins to discuss their feelings, concerns, and aspirations. This practice helps to ensure that both partners feel heard and understood, preventing misunderstandings and fostering deeper connection.

Another important area for joint goals is enhancing intimacy. Couples can work together to rebuild emotional and physical closeness by setting goals around spending time together, being affectionate, and exploring each other's needs and desires. This might include planning regular date nights, taking up shared hobbies, or simply making time to talk and connect without distractions.

Financial planning is another significant aspect of setting future goals as a couple. Financial stress can be a major source of conflict, so establishing clear, mutual goals around saving, spending, and investing can help to create stability and reduce tension. Whether it's saving for a home, planning for retirement, or budgeting for vacations, financial goals provide a clear pathway for working together towards a secure future.

Setting future goals also involves planning for potential challenges. Life is unpredictable, and being prepared for setbacks can help couples navigate difficulties without losing sight of their shared vision. This might include establishing emergency savings, discussing how to handle potential conflicts, or setting up support systems for when times get tough. By anticipating and planning for challenges, couples can strengthen their resilience and maintain their commitment to each other.

Incorporating fun and adventure into goal-setting is equally important. Setting goals around shared interests and new experiences can inject excitement and joy into the relationship. Whether it's traveling to new places, trying out new activities, or learning something new together, these goals create positive, shared memories that strengthen the bond between partners.

Celebrating Milestones in Recovery

Celebrating milestones in recovery is a powerful way to acknowledge progress, reinforce positive behaviors, and motivate continued growth. Recovery from infidelity is a long and often difficult journey, so recognizing and celebrating achievements along the way helps to maintain momentum and positivity.

Milestones in recovery can take many forms. They might include achieving personal goals, such as completing a course of therapy, reaching a fitness target, or overcoming a significant emotional hurdle. They can also encompass relational milestones, such as having a difficult but constructive conversation, re-establishing physical intimacy, or reaching a new level of trust and understanding.

Celebrating these milestones involves more than just acknowledging them; it's about taking time to reflect on the journey, appreciate the effort and progress, and share in the joy of achievement. This reflection helps to reinforce the behaviors and attitudes that contribute to recovery, creating a positive feedback loop that encourages continued effort and growth.

One way to celebrate milestones is through personal rituals. These might include journaling about the achievement, sharing the milestone with a trusted friend or therapist, or engaging in a favorite self-care activity. Personal rituals help to internalize the achievement, making it a meaningful part of the recovery journey.

As a couple, celebrating milestones together is equally important. This might involve planning a special date night, taking a short trip, or simply spending quality time together reflecting on the progress made. Sharing in the joy of achievement strengthens the bond between partners and reinforces their commitment to the relationship.

It's also valuable to mark milestones with tangible rewards. This could be something small, like a favorite treat or a new book, or something more significant, like a weekend getaway. Tangible rewards provide a concrete reminder of the progress made, serving as a motivator for continued effort and growth.

Celebrating milestones also involves expressing gratitude. Taking time to acknowledge and appreciate each other's efforts and contributions fosters a positive, supportive atmosphere. Gratitude can be expressed through words, actions, or small gestures, such as writing a heartfelt note or planning a surprise. This practice of gratitude helps to maintain a focus on the positive aspects of the relationship and the recovery journey, promoting a sense of partnership and mutual support.

Another important aspect of celebrating milestones is sharing them with a supportive community. Whether it's with friends, family, or a support group, sharing achievements creates a sense of connection and validation. It provides an opportunity to receive encouragement and support, reinforcing the progress made and motivating continued effort.

In conclusion, moving forward after infidelity involves setting future goals and celebrating milestones in recovery. By setting individual and joint goals, couples can create a shared vision for the future, fostering unity and purpose. Celebrating milestones along the way helps to acknowledge progress, reinforce positive behaviors, and maintain motivation. Through personal reflection, shared celebrations, tangible rewards, expressions of gratitude, and community support, couples can navigate the journey of recovery, building a stronger, more resilient relationship and embracing a brighter future together.

CONCLUSION

Reflecting on the Journey

The journey of overcoming Post Infidelity Stress Disorder (PISD) is undeniably arduous, marked by moments of intense pain, self-discovery, and profound growth. Reflecting on this journey allows individuals and couples to appreciate the progress they have made and recognize the resilience they have cultivated. The initial shock of discovering infidelity often plunges one into a whirlwind of emotions, from anger and sadness to confusion and betrayal. However, it is through navigating these tumultuous waters that true healing begins.

The path to recovery involves acknowledging and understanding the depth of one's emotions. Identifying the feelings that surface in the wake of infidelity, such as grief, loss, and fear, is the first step towards processing and eventually healing them. This journey is deeply personal and varies for each individual. For some, it might involve seeking therapy, while for others, it may mean turning to trusted friends and family for support. Regardless of the path chosen, the importance lies in confronting these emotions head-on rather than suppressing them.

Throughout this process, personal growth becomes a central theme. The aftermath of infidelity often prompts individuals to re-evaluate their self-worth, beliefs, and priorities. This period of introspection can lead to significant personal development, fostering a stronger sense of self and a clearer understanding of one's needs and boundaries. It is during these times that individuals learn the importance of self-care, self-compassion, and self-respect. Embracing these principles not only aids in personal healing but also contributes to building a healthier and more balanced relationship.

Embracing Hope and Resilience

As the dust begins to settle, embracing hope and resilience becomes crucial. Hope is the beacon that guides individuals through the darkest times, reminding them that better days are ahead. It instills a sense of possibility and optimism, encouraging individuals to keep moving forward despite the challenges they face. Resilience, on the other hand, is the strength that allows individuals to bounce back from adversity. It is the inner fortitude that empowers one to rise after falling, to heal after hurting, and to rebuild after breaking.

Resilience is not an inherent trait but rather a skill that can be developed and strengthened over time. It involves cultivating a positive mindset, practicing mindfulness, and adopting healthy coping mechanisms. Building resilience requires patience and persistence, but the rewards are invaluable. A resilient individual can navigate the complexities of recovery with grace and strength, emerging stronger and more empowered.

Hope and resilience go hand in hand. Together, they create a powerful combination that enables individuals to not only survive infidelity but to thrive in its aftermath. Embracing hope means believing in the possibility of a brighter future, while resilience provides the tools to navigate the journey towards that future. This dual approach allows individuals to heal from the past, live fully in the present, and look forward to the future with confidence and optimism.

Inspirational Stories of Overcoming PISD

Throughout this book, we have explored the many facets of Post Infidelity Stress Disorder and the complex journey of healing and recovery. While the process is challenging, many have successfully navigated this path and emerged stronger, offering hope and inspiration to others facing similar struggles. These stories of resilience and triumph highlight the human capacity for growth and renewal, even in the face of profound betrayal.

One such story is that of Sarah and David. Married for fifteen years, their relationship was rocked by David's infidelity. The discovery left Sarah devastated and questioning the future of their marriage. Through therapy and open communication, they began to address the underlying issues that had contributed to the infidelity. Over time, they were able to rebuild their relationship on a foundation of honesty and trust. Today, Sarah and David are stronger than ever, having transformed their relationship into a partnership rooted in mutual respect and understanding.

Another inspiring journey is that of Lisa, who discovered her partner's infidelity just months after giving birth to their first child. The revelation plunged her into a deep depression, exacerbated by the demands of new motherhood. Determined to heal for herself and her child, Lisa sought therapy and joined a support group for women dealing with infidelity. Through these resources, she found the strength to leave her unfaithful partner and rebuild her life. Lisa's story is a testament to the power of self-love and resilience, illustrating that it is possible to create a fulfilling life even after profound betrayal.

Mark's story provides another perspective on overcoming PISD. After discovering his wife's affair, he initially struggled with feelings of inadequacy and anger. Seeking to understand his emotions and heal, Mark turned to individual therapy and immersed himself in personal development. Through this journey, he discovered a renewed sense of self-worth and confidence. Mark and his wife eventually decided to part ways, but his story highlights the importance of personal growth and self-discovery in the healing process.

These stories, though diverse, share common themes of resilience, hope, and personal growth. They illustrate that while the journey of overcoming PISD is challenging, it is also a journey of profound transformation. Each story underscores the importance of seeking support, whether through therapy, support groups, or trusted loved ones. They also highlight the critical role of self-care and personal development in the healing process.

The journey of overcoming Post Infidelity Stress Disorder is a multifaceted and deeply personal one. Reflecting on the journey allows individuals to appreciate their progress and recognize their resilience. Embracing hope and resilience provides the strength and optimism needed to navigate this challenging path. Inspirational stories of those who have overcome PISD offer hope and encouragement, illustrating that it is possible to heal and thrive after infidelity. As you move forward on your own journey, remember that you have the strength within you to overcome, to heal, and to build a brighter, more fulfilling future.

Appendices

Worksheets for Emotional Processing

Worksheet 1: Identifying Emotions
- **Instructions:** Take some quiet time to reflect on your emotions. Use this worksheet to identify and articulate your feelings.

1. **What emotions am I currently experiencing?**

Example: Anger, sadness, confusion, betrayal, relief.

2. **What triggered these emotions?**

Example: A recent argument, a memory, a conversation.

3. **How do these emotions manifest in my body?**

Example: Tension in the shoulders, headaches, stomachaches.

4. **What thoughts are associated with these emotions?**

Example: "I can't trust anyone," "I'm not good enough," "What if it happens again?"

Worksheet 2: Emotional Regulation Techniques
- **Instructions:** Use this worksheet to explore and practice techniques for regulating your emotions.

1. **Deep Breathing Exercises**

Take a deep breath in for a count of four, hold for four, and exhale for four. Repeat five times.

2. **Grounding Techniques**

Describe five things you can see, four things you can touch, three things you can hear, two things you can smell, and one thing you can taste.

3. **Journaling**

Write about your emotions and experiences for ten minutes without stopping.

4. **Positive Affirmations**

List three positive affirmations to counter negative thoughts.

Worksheet 3: Reflective Journaling Prompts

- **Instructions:** Use these prompts to guide your journaling practice.

1. **What is the hardest part of this journey for me?**
2. **What small victories have I achieved recently?**
3. **How can I practice self-compassion today?**
4. **What am I grateful for in this moment?**

Checklists for Self-Care and Relationship Building

Self-Care Checklist

- Daily Self-Care Activities:

1. Engage in 30 minutes of physical activity.
2. Eat three balanced meals.
3. Drink at least 8 glasses of water.
4. Practice a relaxation technique (e.g., meditation, deep breathing).
5. Spend 15 minutes on a hobby or activity you enjoy.

- Weekly Self-Care Activities:

1. Schedule time for a creative outlet (e.g., drawing, writing, music).
2. Connect with a friend or family member.
3. Spend time in nature or a calming environment.
4. Reflect on personal goals and achievements.
5. Treat yourself to something special (e.g., a favorite meal, a small gift).

Relationship Building Checklist

- Daily Relationship Activities:

1. Express appreciation for your partner.
2. Spend 20 minutes in meaningful conversation.
3. Share a hug or a gesture of affection.
4. Practice active listening without interrupting.
5. Resolve minor conflicts before the end of the day.

- Weekly Relationship Activities:

1. Plan a date night or special activity together.
2. Discuss and align on short-term goals.
3. Reflect on the week's challenges and successes as a couple.
4. Share something new you've learned or experienced.
5. Write a note or message expressing love and gratitude.

Glossary of Terms

Post Infidelity Stress Disorder (PISD): A condition characterized by the emotional and psychological trauma that occurs after discovering infidelity in a relationship. Symptoms can include anxiety, depression, obsessive thoughts, and difficulties in trust and intimacy.

Emotional Regulation: Techniques and strategies used to manage and respond to intense emotions in a healthy and productive manner.

Self-Care: Practices and activities individuals engage in to maintain and improve their physical, emotional, and mental well-being.

Forgiveness: The process of letting go of resentment and anger towards someone who has wronged you, which does not necessarily imply condoning their actions but allows for emotional healing.

Resilience: The ability to recover and bounce back from adversity, stress, or trauma, often involving a positive adaptation in the face of significant challenges.

Intimacy: A close, familiar, and usually affectionate or loving personal relationship with another person. It can be emotional, physical, or both.

Therapy/Counseling: Professional guidance provided by a therapist or counselor to help individuals or couples understand and resolve personal, emotional, or psychological issues.

Support Groups: Groups of people who share similar experiences or concerns and meet regularly to provide mutual support, share information, and offer emotional comfort.

Mindfulness: The practice of maintaining a non-judgmental state of heightened awareness of one's thoughts, emotions, or experiences on a moment-to-moment basis.

Active Listening: A communication technique that involves fully concentrating, understanding, responding, and remembering what is being said during a conversation.

Conflict Resolution: The process of resolving a dispute or disagreement in a peaceful, constructive manner, often involving communication and negotiation skills.